HALFTIME

By

Rick Ebner

PROLOGUE

"EB, YOU USED TO BE SUCH A GOOD ATHLETE...."

In 1981, I was an All-Conference, All-Metro football player who would be inducted into the Bloomington Jefferson High School Hall of Fame. I went to University of Minnesota–Duluth on a football scholarship and wrestled for the Bulldogs. I got married in 1986 at the age of twenty-three, and by the age of forty my wife and I had four beautiful kids—two girls and two boys. They were, and are, the apples of my eye.

When I was twenty-five years old I played on a softball team made up of old high school friends. I had been noticing subtle changes in my body that I was attributing to past athletic injuries.

"Eb, you use to be such a good athlete. What happened?" This

3

was the comment made to me during a softball practice that year. During practices I could not judge fly balls as they flew over my head. One particular play I was protecting third base. As a base runner was about to slide into the base, I was receiving a bullet-thrown softball. I extended my glove and misjudged the ball and it hit me square in the forehead. It left me with a backward Rawlings imprint! And I noticed that while running the bases, my legs were not moving fast like they use to. I couldn't understand what was going on; the athletic skills I had worked on so diligently for twenty years were fading fast! I remember thinking, *I'm getting old, so that is why my skills are decreasing.* I was only twenty-five!

At the age of thirty-two, I was diagnosed with Multiple Sclerosis. My life had been so good. My wife and I were happy and had a three-year-old and a one-year-old. My business was successful.

It's now 2016 and a lot has happened since those innocent days on the softball field. I have become divorced, and I am a motivational speaker, living in a van down by the river. Ha! I love using that old Chris Farley bit from *Saturday Night Live.* Don't worry, I don't really live in a van down by the river.

I am independent, living with my girlfriend, getting around town in my cool power wheelchair, and driving my own adapted van. Yes, life has completely changed for me, but I'm good. Very good. I am still an athlete, and a good one too! I'm an athlete in the Big Game—the game of life.

This book is called *Halftime* because of what you do during halftime in a football game; you make adjustments for the second half. I can't walk, so I use a scooter. I can't drive, so I get hand controls. I can't read small print, so I buy readers. Now, I don't necessarily like all these changes, but in order to succeed in life one must adapt or be left behind.

I have chosen to adapt by living my life according to a set of principles. In fact, the word H-A-L-F-T-I-M-E is an acronym for Humor, Attitude, Love, Faith, Tenacity, Integrity, Movement, and Energy. I try to be intentional about living my life according to these ideals since I find them valuable as I continue on my journey.

I have written this book because I want to share my stories. I want to make my kids proud by having written it. I want all the angels who God sends to be with me to know how much they mean to me. I want others who have been touched by MS to know what it has been like for me. Life is good! I want to share my journey because it may help someone else.

I hope you enjoy these stories, and I hope they encourage you, as you may be one who is "touched by MS."

FAMILY

SAMANTHA SOOTHES THE SOUL

At the time I was diagnosed with MS in 1995, life was busy and I had a lot of responsibilities. I owned my own business and thought I controlled my own destiny. My dad used to say, "There is a lot of money out there, Ricky. It's up to you how much you want to work." I believed that to be true, but sometimes circumstances change and we need to redirect our focus. My world was pretty big at one time with lots of opportunity in the business world. I loved the feeling of being an entrepreneur and building my business. The excitement, feeling important, feeling needed, traveling ... the world was my oyster! I had nice cars, a nice home, four great kids, a pretty wife, and a healthy income.

7

Not surprising, a year after my diagnosis I was dealing with depression. I was in a funk that I couldn't get out of. My family practitioner suggested I talk to a psychologist about how I was feeling. Well, I grew up in a time where we thought only crazy people went to shrinks! He gave me a business card for a local psychologist. It took a while for me to build up enough courage to call and set up an appointment. When I walked into the large medical facility, I started looking for the mental health clinic. Two women standing in the hallway looked at me and asked if they could help me find what I was looking for. I looked down at the business card, embarrassed by the words *mental health clinic*, and replied that I could find it by myself. When I finally found the room, I walked in and saw two women in the waiting room. I thought, *Well, that one's nuts, the other one must be crazy!*

Once in the doctor's office, I noticed a box of tissues sitting on the arm of my chair. *What is this doing here?* I thought. Well, I soon I found out. After my session was over, the box of tissues was empty. The doctor informed me that she thought I was very close to being clinically depressed. I met with her for more than two months, and she gave me some great advice. I started taking antidepressants and got back into life. I decided to volunteer at the Minnesota Masonic Home. It is a nursing home with many other services. Since I got to choose what I did there, I decided to spend time with ladies who had Alzheimer's. I figured that I couldn't do too much harm there.

When I asked the home's director what she would think if I were to bring my five-year-old daughter, Samantha, with me, she thought it was an excellent idea. So for the next eight months Sammy and I went once a week to meet with Thelma (86) and Vera (92). Having

Sammy there took the pressure off of me, as all the ladies wanted to do was spend time with Sam! Volunteering was preventing me from being self-absorbed. I got my eyes off myself and started to do the things that made me happy again—working out, biking, golfing, getting involved in church, being there (mentally) for my two daughters and wife. (I recommend to anyone dealing with any kind of depression to go see someone, talk to someone. Don't isolate yourself. You're not crazy or weird. Life is tough and we all can use some TLC. And good meds!)

ALEX THE BRAVE

In 2000, my oldest daughter, Alex, was six years old and an exceptional bike rider. I brought Alex and her bike with me to Normandale Lake in Bloomington, Minnesota. The path around the lake is a bit more than two miles long. This was a lake that I had run countless times training for 10K races or just out for a leisurely run or walk. This day, I pulled Alex's bike out of my van, strapped on her helmet, and we began our journey. I will never forget that run because I was able to share the experience with Alex. We had made it three-quarters of the way around the lake when my left leg started dragging. Alex could see I was struggling and said, "Dad, we can stop and rest. I don't want you to fall and hurt yourself." She was so sweet and loving. I replied, "No, Alex, I can make it." I was so determined to finish. I wanted to show her how not to give up. We did make it around the lake without stopping! Alex is twenty-one now, and that was the last time I ran around Normandale Lake – or any other lake. Sharing this final experience with my daughter is something I will never forget. Thanks, Alex!

I LOVE MY DAD

My relationship with my dad, Jim Ebner, was unique. I looked up to him and loved him very much. He grew up in Cleveland, Ohio, and had one sister. When he was young he was pretty wild, painting his grandfather's car orange and burning down a barn. His parents were strict. With my grandfather's business (Richard H. Ebner Optical), they could afford to send my dad to military school at Valley Forge Military Academy in Pennsylvania. Dad was big: six feet three inches and 225 pounds. He played football and ran track for Valley Forge. He once beat Olympian Bob Mathias in the 100-meter high hurdles in Madison Square Garden. He went on to earn a football scholarship in 1950 to Ohio State University under legendary coach Woody Hayes.

Dad blew out his knee his sophomore year, and his father died of a heart attack at the age of fifty-four. So Dad dropped out of OSU and went to work at the family business with his mother, Erma. Soon after, they sold the family business, and Dad got involved in the wholesale part of the optical business (eyewear, lenses, and equipment). He and my mom, Henry, were transferred to Minnesota from Ohio in 1965. My father told me that when he got transferred to Minnesota, he didn't know where it was, just that it was cold. My brother, David, was six months old, I was two and one half years old, my sister Amy was eight, and my oldest sister, Suzy, was eleven. With no extended family nearby for support, my parents had their hands full.

I had gotten into the optical business right after I graduated from college. My dad got me a job with his biggest and best customer, Walman Optical. They are the largest independent wholesale optical lab in the country. I started out grinding lenses in their lab making seven dollars an hour. Because of my inside connection, I was being paid two dollars an hour more than anyone else. Within five years I earned a sales position selling eyewear to optical retailers in northern Minnesota and North Dakota. They were not the most glamorous of territories, and were actually quite treacherous in the wintertime, but my customers were so good to me, especially in North Dakota. They appreciated me driving 700 miles to serve them. We developed such good relationships that when I had sales contests within our company I would inform my customers about the contests and they would support me by buying more product. I was competing against reps that travelled New York, Los Angeles, Chicago—much bigger cities than in my territory. I earned trips to Germany and Venice. I loved my job and the customers (friends) I called on.

In 1995, I had been working on my own for about six years when my dad asked me to join his business as a partner. Dad was a manufacturers' representative, and over time grew his business to the point where he needed another person. I worked for him and he taught me about his end of the business, manufacturing. We founded JNR Optics (Jim and Rick) and traveled the country together. He did not like to fly so we drove everywhere: Connecticut, San Antonio, Chicago, St. Louis, Tennessee. We always made room for our golf clubs in the trunk (one of the perks of driving)!

Obviously, my dad was very important to me. I was so proud of him and I knew we were blessed to share so much time together. He told me that he wanted me to have his business when he was gone. After four years of working together he was diagnosed with prostate cancer that had metastasized. He started treatments of hormone injections to slow the progression. He fought it with radiation and chemotherapy. Of course he could not travel with me anymore. I felt the effects of missing him on the road and contemplated life without my dad. *Life will never be the same,* I thought.

The last few months of his life he struggled tremendously with the fear of dying. Depression overtook him and he lost all hope. My dad was like a John Wayne figure to me. Big guy, sometimes intimidating, but always loved to laugh and take money from his golf buddies!

I will never forget one day in 2002 when he came over to my house. He told me he was afraid to die. His hope was gone. The doctors said there was nothing they could do to prevent the cancer from growing and it was near the end for him. I can still hear him telling me, *"Ricky, I can't believe my life is over. It went so fast."* He was in such a hopeless place. I had to say something to him that had been on my mind for a while. I think I asked God for the right words. Then I said, "Dad, I know something that will help you, and you don't have to take another pill for it." I started talking to him about Jesus. He stopped me and said, "I would be a hypocrite if I turned to God now. I lived my life a certain way, and that would not be right."

I tried to explain how when Jesus was on the cross, He was with two other men who were being punished, too. One of the men believed Jesus was the Son of God, and Jesus told him he would be with Him in paradise. But my dad felt unworthy of forgiveness. I asked him to speak to my pastor, Dean Engelbretson. My dad looked at me and said, "I'm not ready for that. That wouldn't be right." He had too much pride. My dad left my house and went home to my mom.

Two days later he called me and said, "I guess I will talk to your pastor friend." I was so excited! I called Pastor Dean, who visited my father. A few days after their meeting I was over seeing my dad, and he said to me, "I guess I'm supposed to get a Bible?" My mom took me aside and said, "Ricky, we have Bibles all over the place." I said, "That's okay, I'll get him one."

My dad died two months later. He was my best friend and I looked up to him. This was the toughest and proudest time in my life. I had the opportunity to witness to my dad. Now I know where he is!

It dawned on me, we can learn from our parents all the way until the end of their lives. This experience showed me how important faith is. My dad was a very strong man, but when he got sick and was walking without faith, he became scared and felt alone. This reaffirms to me that I need the Lord now to get through these tough times. And we don't need to worry about feeling unworthy or hypocritical; Jesus died on the cross to take all that away.

Never Been a Quitter

In 2007, my wife, Sue, and I made a difficult decision. We decided it was time for me to go on Social Security Disability. My mother had passed away in January of 2006. The stress of going through her battle with lung cancer and running JNR Optics was just too daunting for me to continue. The stress was affecting my MS; my left leg was dragging and I was unable to lift my left foot. When extreme stress would hit, my thinking became cloudy and I was indecisive. I was told by my doctors that going on disability would be the smartest thing to do for my health. That might have been true, but the most difficult thing up to this point was calling to tell my vendors, my customers, my family, and my friends. It felt like I was quitting and letting MS win.

NIGHTMARE ON CANTERBURY DRIVE

Even though we started out happy, seasons changed, and Sue and I were divorced in 2008.

Springtime of 2010, I was moving to a nice rambler with my four kids, whom I had for 50% of the time. I stopped over to the house to meet with the landlady. As I walked up to the house using my cane, I caught my toe on the cement and fell. I landed square on my nose and forehead. It felt like my nose was shoved up into my face. As I lay facedown, I was seeing white flashes, and blood was coming out of my nose. I was right at the front door. A small pool of blood amassed as I strained to get to my feet. I was groggy and thought it best not to ring the doorbell. I did not want to scare this poor woman with my bloodied face. I drove over to a neighbor's house, where they helped me with towels, water, and a place to rest. I went to the hospital the next day and it was determined I had a concussion and a broken nose.

At this time, I was very involved in my kids' activities, because I could be. Being on disability gave me the freedom to spend quality time with them. This particular day, I had signed Jimmy (9) up for soccer and Jack (7) for football. Being unorganized, I realized it was the last day for sign-ups. Typically, Sue and I discussed activities for the boys. This time I did not communicate with her because of the tight time frame. That was my mistake.

What happened the next day when she came over to my house to pick up Jim and Jack was unimaginable. I so regret handling the situation the way I did. Our fourteen-year-old daughter, Alex, was in the front seat of Sue's car as they pulled up into the driveway. Sue got out of the car and we started talking about how the week went. Everything was cordial until I told her I had signed the boys up for fall sports, and their first practices started that night. She had just arrived from out of town, and I was telling her she needed to take the boys to their first practices. She told me she would not take them. She was upset with me because I didn't talk with her about the boys being signed up for sports. I told her that the boys could stay with me and I would take them to their first practices.

We stood outside her car and argued. The argument got worse and I told her to leave my property. She would not leave, so I threatened to call the police. I realized I had left my cell phone in the house. Using my cane, I walked to my front door, while Sue followed me. I opened the screen door and proceeded to open my storm door when I noticed she was right there holding the screen door open. I tried to close the storm door three times with my left hand, which is considerably weaker due to the MS. She blocked the door from closing each time. My storm door had small square windows on the top half of the door as its design. As she stood holding the screen door open, I repositioned my cane so I could use my strong arm. I slammed the door harder, and she put her hand out to stop the door from closing. What happened next left us both shocked. Her hand and arm went through the window. I saw beads of blood appear on her arm. I said immediately, "I'm calling the police!" She said the same thing and within five minutes two squad cars were there.

After the police questioned us, they determined I was at fault. They informed me of my rights and arrested me. I have never been arrested in my life. I never intended her arm to go through the window, I just did not want her in my house. I asked the officers if they could cuff me with my hands in front so I could use my cane. They agreed. As we walked across the front yard I noticed my neighbors were outside watching the excitement. This was so very surreal.

I told the officers, "I need my meds from my house." My injections for the MS and Coumadin (blood thinner) for my blood clots. After they put me in the back of the squad car, they entered my house and gathered my medicine.

I sat in disbelief. How can this be happening to me?

When we got to the police station, we entered a room where I was fingerprinted and got a "glamour shot." They had me change into something very similar to the hospital gown I was wearing one month earlier. (I'll explain that story later in the book.) They put me in a cell by myself—thank goodness—with a blanket and pillow. As I sat on my bed looking at the stainless steel toilet, I remembered there was an important Twins game I was going to miss. It was the Twins versus the White Sox to make it into the playoffs. There was an intercom button I could press to talk to the officers if I needed anything, so I would ask for updates on the score of the game. Being in sales for so many years, I knew how important it was to be friendly with everyone, so I befriended the guards. I was not trying to be manipulative; it's just my nature. So I would press my call button and get updates on the score of the Twins game all night long.

I asked the officers if I could have another blanket because it was chilly in my cell. They complied and even brought an extra pillow for me since no one else was spending the night in jail. Lucky me. When it was time for dinner I heard a knock at my door and a plate was shoved through my slot. It was a microwaved cheeseburger with a bag of potato chips. As I started to open and eat my burger, it occurred to me that one month ago I was being served dinner by pretty nurses while lying in bed, remote control in hand, and medicine being pumped into me. I smiled and took a bite of my burger.

As the night progressed, I started to feel very lonely. I had arrived at 3:00 p.m. and now it was 10:30 p.m. There was a knock on my door. The officer opened my cell and told me I had visitors. I put the blanket over my shoulder to keep off the chill and went to the visiting area. A plexiglass barrier separated us. It was my sister Suzy and her husband. As I was about to sit down, I painfully grabbed my buttocks and said to them, "I have a rough roommate!" I proceeded to giggle and let them know I had my own cell. They laughed.

After we talked for a while and I explained what happened, I became very emotional. It finally hit me. When they left I walked back to my cell, lay down on the one-inch-thick pad, and pulled the two sheets up over my head, thinking, *I can't wait to wake up and get out of here!*

The morning came, and I was happy to have the night over with. The commander of the police department came and saw me. I had requested to speak to him the night before, but he was not in. I knew him from Caribou Coffee. We had chatted quite a few times. We had gone to the same high school, even though he was a few years older than me. When he entered, I was both comforted and embarrassed. I asked him questions about what had happened to me with the arrest. He reiterated to me, "The officers did what they were supposed to do. It was protocol."

The commander led me out of my cell to process my departure. I had to sign the paperwork and that's when I saw my mug shot. I had just had a haircut and I was tan from being outside. It was a nice picture, so I asked if I could get a copy of it. The officers stopped what they were doing and gave me a look. They didn't say anything, so I did not push it.

My brother, David, picked me up to bring me home. It was so good to be going home. I talked to my brother about the whole ordeal as we cleaned the broken glass from the storm door. I had just experienced a very stressful time and I was okay! I thought to myself, *What an experience! I just spent the night in jail!*

One week after the incident, I attended the Friday night football game at my old high school. I bumped into a police officer I knew who was working the game. I told him my experience of being arrested and asked if he could get a copy of my mug shot. "Let me see what I can do," he answered. Less than a week later my mug shot arrived in the mail.

About the same time, I received a letter from child protection services informing me that a restraining order had been issued to me. This meant I could not see my children until we had a court hearing. This was so upsetting for me. I felt beaten down. Earlier that day I had a visit from my social worker, Heather from the MS Society. It had been a while since I had met with her. I explained about my five blood clots, being arrested, spending the night in jail, and now having a restraining order against me. Talk about drama! Heather looked at me and asked if I had ever contemplated suicide? I looked at her and said, "No, but do you think I should be?"

She kind of giggled but was dead serious. I assured her, "No, it has not crossed my mind." She was doing her job, making sure I was not in a dangerous state of mind. I understood that. She also told me some people plan out their suicide. I had no idea people did this. But what did happen was that a tiny seed was planted in my mind.

Later that week, on a Friday night at about 10 p.m., I bought a pack of cigarettes, grabbed a beer, and went to my garage. I'm not a smoker, but I was at an emotional low point. I sat in a chair and started to cry, then sobbed. I sat there and analyzed my life: both Mom and Dad had passed away, I was divorced, restrained from my kids, forced to sell my home, let go of my business, was living on Social Security Disability, was fighting a chronic disease – no longer able to walk, run, bike, golf. And the biggest loss: choosing to walk away from my Lord.

I sat there feeling so down. Soon, the seed that was planted in my mind while meeting with Heather came alive. I remember sitting back in my chair looking up at the rafters and evaluating the beam. Looking at that beam caused me to think of getting a rope, but I had no rope. I was renting this house. I looked through my garage and saw rope. I would need a ladder. And sure enough, I looked to my right and there was a ladder. I was picturing myself taking the ladder.

Everything was coming together. I had the rafter beam, the rope, and now the ladder. I was sobbing and visualizing my suicide. The garage door was open (subconsciously, so someone might see me). I saw myself with the noose around my neck and stepping off the ladder, but there was someone there grabbing me around the waist and preventing me from dying.

There was a spiritual warfare going on in my mind. It felt like I had Satan on one shoulder telling me to do it. He was saying, "You're worthless. Do it! No one cares about you." On my other shoulder was God trying to speak to me, but I was so down and fixated on myself that I didn't listen. I got up from the chair and walked with my cane to where the rope was hanging. I grabbed the rope and sat down in my chair. As I attempted to create a noose, it dawned on me that I hadn't participated in Boy Scouts or Cub Scouts, so I didn't know how to tie that type of knot.

About that moment my phone rang. It was my dear friend Tom Mould. We were in Bible study class together and I looked up to him as a man of integrity and godliness. He never calls me—especially on a Friday night at 10:00. He could tell I was upset. I reassured him everything was okay and told him I would talk to him later. I kind of blew him off. I was on a mission, trying to make a slip knot and end things. Because my left hand is affected by the MS, I struggled even more.

After about ten minutes, I successfully accomplished my noose and slipped it over my head. As tears were running down my cheeks, I sat there feeling so defeated, scared, and tired. I had never been to this place before. Never this hopeless. I wanted to do it, but I didn't want to. The spiritual battle was real and my life was on the line. My phone was sitting in front of me on a table. I reached over and dialed Tom back. For those of you who know Tom Mould, you know he is a man of strong faith but does not typically answer his phone. Well, he did answer the phone this time. I told Tom, "I'm in a bad place." He could tell I was upset and kept me on the phone until he showed up in my driveway.

Tom walked into the garage, saw the rope around my neck, and said, "That's a silly-looking tie!" He helped me take it off. Tom was with me for the next hour talking to me and praying. I listened to him. I was so exhausted. I knew what he was saying but I couldn't just snap my fingers and be happy or thankful. After Tom left, I went to bed and slept ten hours. I needed it!

I woke up and started to analyze what I went through in the garage. It did not take long to understand why I contemplated suicide. I had walked away from the Lord. I tried doing it—life—on my own. I thought about being in the hospital with the five blood clots, being arrested and in jail, the restraining order preventing me from seeing my kids, and my MS progressing and preventing me from living the life I once had. None of those things caused me to put a rope around my neck. I realized when I walked away from the Lord, I was walking away from HOPE, LOVE, JOY ... LIFE! The rope around my neck represented anger, hopelessness, resentment, selfishness, and DEATH!

I truly believe the Lord does miracles every day through people. He uses people to give hope, joy, and love to those who are hurting. I have learned to ask Him to use me, to make a difference in other people's lives. I try to do this daily through prayer.

JACK SOCKS IT TO ME

One day in the summer of 2012, as I sat on the side of my bed attempting to put on my socks, I became fatigued. MS fatigue is different than normal fatigue. It can totally wipe you out for twenty minutes to several days, depending on the activity and how far along you are with MS. My son Jack, who was ten years old, watched me struggle. I dropped my socks to the floor after the fifth attempt. I lay back on my bed frustrated and tired. Jack walked over to me, picked up my socks, and started putting them on my feet. My first feeling was anger. Not at Jack but at the fact that my ten-year-old son was having to help his father get dressed.

My emotions changed quickly as I asked Jack, "What are you thinking right now? How do you feel?" Jack looked up with his big blue eyes and said with a smile, "I feel really good, Dad! I get to help my dad! None of my friends get to help their dads like me." I looked at him with such pride, astonishment, and love. I realized something good coming from this ugly disease: Jack has acquired something special not easily found in most people, let alone a ten-year-old boy. He has compassion and kindness!

That same summer, Jack and I purchased the movie *Marley & Me* about a family dog that becomes a nuisance because he constantly gets into trouble. Eventually the dog gets older and becomes sick, then the father of the family has the unbearable task of putting Marley down. As you can imagine, this is a heartrending scene. As Jack and I watched, I noticed him holding back tears. I looked at Jack and said, "It's okay, Jack. It's okay to cry." I held him and he cried on my shoulder uncontrollably for about five minutes.

I will never forget that moment because of what happened two weeks later. My daughter, Alex, had her senior prom pictures being held outside. It was particularly hot that day. Since dealing with MS, heat is my enemy. (It is like Kryptonite to Superman! I become so fatigued I can barely lift my arm or move my body. It's unlike anything I have ever experienced. It's a different fatigue than what you feel after a hard workout. I guess the closest thing I can compare it to is having the flu without being sick to your stomach.) I drove my white Suburban to the area where the pictures were taking place. I attempted to get out of my truck and get on Big Red, my first scooter, but my body would not allow me to. The fatigue hit. Hard! I tried and tried to get out of my truck, but I couldn't. My son Jack came to my aid because he had seen how much I was struggling. I was becoming emotional and frustrated. I wanted to experience Alex's prom pictures and I couldn't do it. Jack got up close to me, looked at me, and said, "Dad, it's okay. It's okay to cry." He put his arms around me and patted me on the back, saying, "It's okay." Wow! My twelve-year-old son was consoling me!

VICTIM OR VICTOR?

In the spring of 2014 I contacted Senior Abilities Unlimited owner, Nicole Rennie. I set up an appointment with Nicole for a home safety evaluation because I was falling more frequently, and I wanted to make sure I was safe. I was walking her through my apartment using my walker when she told me to sit down. She said, "Rick, there are some things I can recommend for you, but can I do a physical therapy session with you first?"

Nicole worked on me for forty-five strenuous minutes, then we sat down and talked. She saw my enthusiasm and she knew I wanted to get better. She went over all the details, but I knew I was not going to be able to afford her wonderful service. After informing Nicole of that, she told me, without hesitation, "I will work with you pro bono." I was floored. She explained, "I can't walk away from someone who exudes hope." My face lit up with a big smile and I thanked her. I can't believe how many kind people there are in this world.

Nicole scheduled me twice a week, for 45-minute sessions. She worked with me for the next two months and eventually had to pass me off to another physical therapist. Her business was growing and her time was sparse; she needed to find someone to fill in for her. Nicole chose her most experienced therapist, Lisa. Lisa is a straight shooter and takes her job very seriously. When I met Lisa, I thought she was attractive and I noticed she was not wearing a wedding ring. She worked with me for about two months when I finally had the courage to ask her out on a date. Initially, she refused my invitation because it was against her professional ethics to date a patient, but I reminded her that I wouldn't be her patient for much longer; we were almost done with my therapy. Well, I'm not sure if it was my charming personality, my full head of hair, or my dimple that finally convinced her, but after my treatment she eventually agreed to go out with me. Actually, I couldn't take her out because my car was being repaired from one of my accidents. I asked her over to my apartment to watch a movie. She accepted my invitation and actually brought me flowers! I don't think I have ever received flowers from a girl before. I thought that was so cool! We hit it off right away, and we have been together for almost two years.

In August of 2015, I had a little issue with my power wheelchair. I was trying to transfer from my smaller wheelchair, Betty Lou, to my big power wheelchair. I was standing up and holding on to my countertop for balance. The chair was a little too far back for me to sit down into it, so I had to reach back while standing and grab the joystick to move it closer to me. I didn't realize the chair was on high speed, and when I pulled the joystick toward me, it shot forward and crushed my legs. I fell to the ground in pain, not able to move. My phone was on the countertop so I couldn't call for help. I knew Lisa was coming over for dinner within an hour, so I relaxed, prayed, and wondered how badly I had hurt my ankle. I thought I sprained it.

When Lisa arrived and saw me on the floor, I looked up at her and said, "How you doin'?" with a smile. She was not amused. She quickly found an extra person to help me up and into my chair. I tested out my leg by putting some weight on it and pain shot through my leg. "No! Not my leg!" X-rays confirmed it was broken. My goal of walking every day to get stronger had been hijacked. My independence was threatened big time. After we got home from the hospital, Lisa and I tested my ability to transfer from my power wheelchair to my bed. I could not do it by myself; Lisa had to help me. Once I was in bed, I could not get out of bed by myself; Lisa had to help me. I could no longer get into the shower, stand while showering, or get dressed; Lisa had to help me. I am so blessed! I know I would have had to move into a transitional center or nursing home if it had not been for Lisa. I was in my cast for roughly twelve weeks, and my legs had definitely atrophied and gotten weaker. I knew I had a big challenge ahead of me. Walking again would take much time and patience. But I had a lot of things going for me. I was already eating well on the Paleo Diet. My mind was healthy because of Christ in my life. And I had the love and companionship of Lisa.

During that time, my sons, Jack and Jim, had been living with me, and we had planned to join Lisa and her whole extended family on their annual summer trip to Yogi Park in Wisconsin. It had been planned for months before my fall and broken leg. And it would be the last quality time I would have with Jimmy and Jack before they permanently moved to Stoughton, Wisconsin, with their mother and stepfather. We made the trip work by staying in a wheelchair-accessible villa. Between sponge baths and being rolled into the pool, I stayed clean, fresh, and pain free. And we all had a blast!

As the trip ended, I said good-bye to my boys and Lisa and I drove back to Minneapolis. Not only was rehabilitation after my broken leg a setback, being apart from my sons was very difficult. But it had gotten harder for me to care for all their needs. Moving to Stoughton with their mom was something they wanted to try. I knew it was right to let them go, but holy cow! It was tough. I was afraid of what my life would be like without my boys here. I remember sitting at my kitchen table and thinking, *I have a choice in how I am going to live my life. I can play the victim or the victor. I chose victor!*

JIMMY THE STRONG

Jimmy, my oldest son, named after my dad, is a fifteen-year-old boy whom I adore. He has such a competitive nature, he reminds me of myself. When Jim was younger he would always be there cheering on his dad, or participating in events like the MS root beer float day or the MS Walk. I would bring Jimmy and Jack into the MS Society in downtown Minneapolis from time to time. All the women in the office thought the boys were adorable. Jimmy developed a crush on a woman and one day brought her some freshly pulled dandelions. Such a charmer!

Sometimes it has been hard for Jim having a dad on a scooter. It can be embarrassing. Other kids didn't have a dad that can't throw a football or play catch with them. I wanted so badly to do the things with Jimmy that my dad did with me! I ended up going to his grade school a lot and even participated in one of his classes. After lunch, I would give him rides on my scooter. His classmates thought he was lucky, and they all wanted rides. Soon the principal asked me to stop giving Jimmy rides. I guess we were disruptive in the hallways. Now that I think about it, I shouldn't have let him steer or control the speed.

I believe Jimmy has developed strength of character, kindness, and compassion, partially from having to deal with the fact that I am living with MS. I believe there is always something good that comes from bad situations. It can be painful, but if we persevere and trust God we will see the good. Jimmy has always been one of my good things.

DADDY'S GIRLS

When Samantha was a very young girl of two or three years of age, she was afraid of everything. I would walk with her outside our house and she would see her shadow and start crying. A breeze would blow by, and she would stop in her tracks and have a conniption. Forget it during the holidays when she'd see Santa or the Easter Bunny. She would have this look of horror on her face and freak out. She was adorable!

Both Sam and Alex remember when I could bike and pull them in their bike trailer. I coached both girls in soccer and softball when they were eight and nine years old. I loved having two little girls. I think every man who has the opportunity to raise daughters is given a blessing and a curse. You love these daddy's girls so much. You protect them and put the fear of God into the boy that asks your little girl out on her first date. I remember shaking these boys' hands when being introduced, squeezing harder and longer than normal, and looking into their eyes with a bit of disdain.

Sam and Alex finished their first MS 150 bike ride during the summer of 2015. I am so proud of my girls. The dream of biking this event together may not be a reality right now, but walking each one down the wedding isle is. I am going to the Courage Center working out on a special bike designed for people that have issues using their legs. I have physical therapy twice a week and am walking using a cane and holding on to my physical therapist's hand. I'm up to about 200 feet with assistance. My goal is to walk fifty feet with my cane in my right hand while gently holding my daughter's hand with my left hand. I say "gently" because my physical therapist has scar marks from me digging my nails into her hand trying to walk. No matter if I can walk them down the isle or they sit on my lap and we go in style, I will be smiling, grateful and thankful that I have the blessing to give my daughters away.

No, Amy, You're Worse Than Me!

My sister Amy, who is five years older than me, is also struggling with MS. Studies have confirmed that there is a genetic MS link within families, yet they still do not know how one develops the disease. Amy's condition is completely different than mine, which is always the case. No two cases of MS are the same. Her MS affects her cognitive and walking abilities. Amy and I have a special bond. We love and care about each other immensely.

Amy recently lost her husband and caregiver of over twenty-five years. We, her siblings, Suzy, David, and I had the daunting task of finding her a new home. We are blessed to have David's wife, Joan, to tackle the project.

Not too long ago I brought Amy over to my apartment for a visit. She is very unstable when she walks, and gets around by shuffling her feet. Not only that, but her memory is affected quite substantially. Our conversations are interesting and, I have to say, humorous at times. At my apartment, Amy watched me struggle as I transferred from one scooter to another. She exclaimed to me how bad she felt for me, and stated it was unfair that I was in worse shape than she is. I shot back at her, "No, Amy, you're worse than me!" We actually started arguing about who was in worse shape. It was comical! We both laughed about the conversation, but ultimately we agree that MS sucks!

ANGELS

Every morning I get out of bed, shower, have coffee, and spend time with the Lord. I read from my daily devotional book called, *Jesus Calling,* by Sarah Young. This is so important to me and enjoyable for me. Spending time in the Word and praying each morning has led me to a world of hope and love. I thank Jesus for everything He has given me, and I ask Him to use me to make a difference in other people's lives.

That's why I believe that fighting MS with my cane, walker, or power wheelchair has given me the opportunity to plant God's seeds by asking for help when the time is right. When someone opens a door for me, I tell that person they are the first angel in my day. Calling someone my angel has become an automatic response whenever people help me. At Caribou, someone brings my coffee to my table, so they are my second angel of the day. The person who helps me reach something on a high shelf at the grocery store is my third angel of the day. And so on. I look right into their eyes and smile with sincerity and gratitude. 99% of the time I receive a smile or a, "God bless you," right back. God blesses all of us with angels. It's up to us to recognize His presence, seek His love, and pass it on.

MOSH PIT MANIA

In the summer of 2001, when I was thirty-nine years old, my child-hood friend Bernie Kaiser picked me up on a Friday night. He was driving a 1971 nitro neon green Bronco convertible and blasting Bruce Springsteen. My girls, Sammy (9) and Alex (7), followed me out to this loud and some would say obnoxious-looking sight. They thought the Bronco was cool and wanted a ride. I kissed them good night. I climbed into the outspoken Bronco and sped away with the music blaring, the top off, and my conservative neighbors looking out their windows. We were heading to Downtown Minneapolis to the nightclub called First Avenue. A favorite local band was playing, and Bernie had invited me to go with him. To say I felt a little out of my comfort zone was an understatement. Driving down the highway, shades on, top off, music cranked, neon green Bronco—well, we were drawing some attention. I was thirty-nine years old with three kids, a wife, a dog, a business, and a home in the suburbs. Time to let my hair down!

As Bernie and I were paying for our tickets, I looked into the nightclub and saw the dance floor. It looked like to me a big brawl was taking place with about fifty people. I pointed it out to Bernie and he explained to me that it was a mosh pit. *A mosh pit?* I thought. *I've seen those on MTV!* (A mosh pit is when a group of people gather on a dance floor and literally slam into each other in a "fun" manner, typically holding and drinking a beer.) I decided right then that before I turned forty, or became physically unable, I was going to experience a mosh pit. It was instantly added to my bucket list!

Bernie and I ordered a couple beers and were enjoying the band. My attention kept going back to the mosh pit where both men and women were having a great time slamming into each other in a somewhat controlled way. We were just about finished with our beers when Bernie looked at me and said, "Are you ready?" I said yes, and off we went to the so-called dance floor. Bernie and I are not small guys, so I was a little concerned about whether I would injure any of the women. Well, we both jumped in and there I was, experiencing my first mosh pit.

I soon realized we were easily the oldest people out there. It didn't matter; we were having a great time. The women were definitely more physical than the guys. After about twenty minutes I needed a break because my legs were feeling a little fatigued. We sat down and had a couple more beers. We laughed and decided we would go back out one more time. I knew I would never be doing this again.

I jumped back into the pit, ready to mix it up. I started getting knocked around like a pinball. My once physically gifted body was being hammered by women I would normally open doors for. Before I knew it, I hit the ground. It seemed like it happened in slow motion. My legs had become very weak and I lay there for about ten seconds. A tall, buxom blonde bent down to help me up. She grabbed me by the shoulders and hoisted me to my feet. As I stood there regaining my composure, she gave me a high five and said, "Fellow moshers stick together!"

Moving Violations

For fifteen years I was blessed to ride in the MS 150. Lots of time spent on my bike raising money for the MS Society to help individuals and families living with MS. It was an incredible event that I loved and cherished each June. My first year, my team was just my insurance man and me. It grew each year with close friends from grade school, high school, and college. My wife, Sue, was our social director. During the ride she would make Bloody Marys for some of us to enjoy at the rest stops. I don't think it was legal. That's how we came up with our team name: Moving Violations. After fifteen years, the team had grown to over eighty people!

When year thirteen came, I didn't think I could do it. This was a very difficult time. It was just another physical activity I could no longer do. Each spring, my good friend Bob Rykken would come over and train with me. I was going to have to tell Bob I thought I was done, that my legs just couldn't do it anymore. Instead of accepting defeat, Bob showed up with a tandem bike! He said, "Let's give this a try." Bob, my brother David, Wes, Mark, and Scott decided to surprise me and bought me a tandem bike.

By the time I was riding the tandem bike, I needed help getting on and off the bike. This meant extreme caution and quite a few hands. The MS 150 is a two-day event, biking 75 miles each day, along with 4,000 other cyclists. The men on our team alternated biking with me (pulling my 200 pounds). It was incredible! I could feel the love that exuded from not only our team, Moving Violations, but all 4,000 riders.

2010 was the first year I was unable to bike in the MS 150, even on my tandem. I had been riding and raising money for MS for fifteen years. I always prided myself in being one of the top fund-raising participants. Now I speak for the MS Society and promote this incredible event. I talk about living life with no regrets, and taking chances and living life abundantly. I embrace life, and it leads to so much thankfulness.

BIG RED AND RAT POISON

Well into my diagnosis and after my divorce, I was dating a woman who was eighteen years younger than me. Jane was fun and attractive, and some of my buddies were actually envious of me! She did not have a relationship with the Lord, but I was drawn to her because I didn't want to be alone. I thought I deserved to have fun with her. We were friends with benefits. I had shared a lot with my men's group at church (about my indiscretions) and they did not support my relationship with Jane. I decided to walk away from church and my men's group.

During this time, my niece Christy who lives in Chicago, was getting married. By now, I typically used a cane to help me get around, but my ability to walk longer distances had become too difficult and required a scooter. This was a very difficult reality for me to accept. There I was, forty-seven years old, sometimes being likened to David Hasselhoff, and dating a girl eighteen years younger than me. This scooter did not fit the picture! But I needed it and decided to name it Big Red.

We drove into Chicago and went directly to Lake Michigan. I lowered Big Red out of my Suburban and surveyed the path we would explore. It was a beautiful summer day and the lake was busy with runners, bikers, and walkers. Jane decided to sit on my lap (I may have suggested the idea). We started riding along the lake; it was beautiful. People got a kick out of seeing the two of us cruising along the lakeshore. There were plenty of thumbs ups and positive comments directed at the two of us. It was a lot of fun! We must have travelled four or five miles like that—enjoying each other, the scenery, and the attention.

We stayed in Chicago for the wedding and did some shopping as well. My scooter was my means of transportation the entire weekend. I still used my cane when I was indoors or going short distances, but I used Big Red a lot while exploring Chicago.

On Sunday we loaded up Big Red and drove the six hours home to Minneapolis. As I drove, I thought about my new experience with the scooter. It wasn't as bad as I had thought it would be. Sure, I noticed the looks I was receiving, but I truly enjoyed the ability to go and do things I could no longer do—long walks, shopping, sight-seeing, being outside. I decided I enjoyed my newfound independence. Plus, I realized there could be some real benefits to this whole "ride share" experience!

The next week home I started to notice a throbbing and pain in my left calf. I didn't think too much of it, until my leg collapsed under my weight a couple times. I decided I should probably go get it checked out by my general practitioner. I figured it had something to do with MS. When you have MS, whenever there are aches or pains, you attribute them to the disease.

Dr. Payne (yes, that is his real name) listened to my heartbeat in my left calf and all the way up my leg with a stethoscope. He ordered an ultrasound and called the hospital to set up the procedure. The radiologist scanned the bottom of my left calf and within two minutes announced I was being admitted. She detected three blood clots going up my left leg—one in my calf, one in my inner thigh, and one in my left buttocks. I was stunned!

They admitted me on the spot. Because of the danger that a blood clot could travel to my lungs or brain they put me on Coumadin (blood thinner) right away. I was put in a private room and my family was contacted. My brother, David, kindly went to my home and gathered all the things I would need for my hospital stay, including my MS medications.

Later that night, they woke me at 1:00 a.m. for more tests. They X-rayed my lungs. By this time, I was pretty out of it and they inserted my body into a CAT Scan tube. They asked me to hold my breath three or four times. Each time I experienced light-headedness. I was returned to my room, and the doctor told me I had two more blood clots in my lungs. My condition could have led to major stroke or death. Hearing that news at two in the morning was shocking!

I stayed in the hospital for over a week. It took that much time for the doctors to get my blood level to a point where it was safe from clotting again. The doctors and nurses were great. I told the nurses I was going to be their favorite patient on the floor and cracked jokes to make the hospital staff smile. I felt blessed that the doctors were able to diagnose my situation so quickly. *Just another bump in the road!* I thought. They actually thought I was not taking my diagnosis very seriously and reminded me about how close to death I had come. I guess I was using some sort of defensive tactic to cope with my fear.

The doctors prescribed Coumadin for the rest of my life. Coumadin is basically rat poison that somehow thins your blood. For a time, I went in twice a week for blood testing to make sure my blood was thin enough to prevent blood clots but not too thin to produce other side effects.

RECONNECTING WITH AL TACHOVSKY

During the summer of 2010, I reconnected with a childhood friend through Facebook, Al "Tack Hammer" Tachovsky. We played Little League Baseball and high school football together. Al was one grade ahead of me in school, so we weren't tight friends. In fact, the last time I had seen Al was playing college football against each other in 1983. I was a running back for he University of Minnesota–Duluth and Al was an All-American linebacker for Minnesota State University–Mankato. He went on to play for the Minnesota Vikings for one year, until he blew out his knee, which ended his football career. Al actually wrestled professionally for three years under the name of "Playboy Allen West" from Zuma Beach, California.

We set up a coffee date at the local IHOP restaurant to get caught up with each other. We sat and talked for over three hours! He had no idea I was battling MS, and I had no idea he was a recovering alcoholic. We sat and shared our personal struggles and how we each coped with our individual diseases.

The one common denominator we shared was our belief in Jesus Christ. Al explained to me that before he accepted the Lord he struggled every Christmas. He would attend Christmas services every year, but it didn't really mean anything to him. Al explained how emotional he would be every Christmas Eve. He would isolate himself and become depressed for no reason he could understand. This occurred while Al was in the midst of his battle with alcohol. His drinking was affecting his marriage and all aspects of his life.

Depression crept in, as well as anger. Al was separated from his wife, Sandy, and two daughters, and he knew he had to change. At the age of thirty-nine, he moved back home with his mother and father. He wanted to change. He read books about relationships, anger management, started attending Alcoholics Anonymous, and tried to make positive changes so he could reunite with Sandy and his daughters, Christy and Taylor.

Al used to sit at the breakfast table each morning and read the newspaper. One particular week he kept seeing an article about an upcoming event to be held at the Metrodome in Downtown Minneapolis. It was for men who wanted to become closer to God. Al saw this advertisement repeatedly every day for a week. The seed was planted in his mind. The event was called Promise Keepers.

Al was intrigued and oddly drawn to go to the event. He sheepishly walked into the Metrodome by himself and headed to the farthest seat, not wanting anyone to notice him. He could not believe there were so many men at this Christian event. They sang worship songs and heard well-known men of faith speak. It was overwhelming to Al, but something was happening. He felt the presence of the Holy Spirit and accepted the Lord into his life. The next day, Al woke up and the urge to drink was gone. It has been fifteen years since he has had a drink, and Al credits everything to that day at Promise Keepers. In my eyes, Al is an amazing husband, father, and role model to everyone.

I don't think it was a coincidence that we reconnected after thirty years. We both had so much to say to each other. We both had gone through tough times but we persevered. We sat and listened to each other's story and laughed a lot.

Al has traveled with me to doctor appointments, numerous visits to the NIH clinic in Bethesda, Maryland, and we have attended church together. Al helped me spiritually when I was struggling by helping me see that I am a "victor not a victim." He's made so many visits to the bathroom to help me, I can't count them all! From helping me on to airplanes to helping me get dressed, picking me up when I have fallen and even tucking me into bed, Al has been there for me. I love you, Al!

When Al was appointed as the event coordinator for the MS Birdie Bash and Dinner Event, he told me he would take the event to the next level. With the drive and tenacity that he applies to his football, wrestling, and sobriety, I had no doubt. Al and I attended a golf show at the Minneapolis Convention Center in 2011. We were in search of donations from various vendors at the show. We had success with people donating items and free weekend stays at courses in northern Minnesota. We had fun approaching different companies with our genuine request. We had great results and realized there are a lot of people that have been "touched by MS." They may have had a family member or friend that was affected by this ugly disease.

When Al and I were leaving the event, we had to pass through security. The security officer was an attractive African-American woman. She and I struck up a conversation and I thought she might have a thing for me. As I was driving away on my scooter, she called for me to come back. I did and she handed me her personal card. I was so tickled! My self-esteem was low because I wasn't feeling like a desirable man. Never had I been hit on while driving my scooter! But I thought, *I still have it!*

As and I was driving us home, I handed Al her card and asked him to read her name. He started laughing uncontrollably. "She's a hooker!" Al shouted. Her title was "Personal Escort." When Al finally finished reading her card, I did not believe him. He laughed even more as I defended her, saying, "That's not true. I think she really likes me." He gave me her card, and when I saw the toll-free number I was crushed. Oh well, she wasn't that pretty anyway.

After my fifteenth year of riding in the MS 150, I was the one who needed help. This is how the Birdie Bash originally started. Now going into our fifth MS Birdie Bash, Al has led our event to amazing heights. We sell out every year with 144 golfers and another 100 or more people for dinner, with silent and live auctions. Special guests include Minnesota Vikings Cheerleaders, University of Minnesota Cheerleaders, Goldy Gopher, Moon from the KS95 Moon & Staci show, and Tony Oliva from the Minnesota Twins. Thanks to Al, we are now growing enough that we are granting funds to help others with MS.

I am so blessed to have so many people who care about me, my family, and others affected by MS. If you're interested in our event, please check out our website at www.MSBirdieBash.org.

PRAY MORE

In 1976 I was in eighth grade. I played in all the sports that were available to me: football, wrestling, baseball, track, and basketball. Schoolwork always came second and it showed in my grades. This particular season it was football, my favorite. I was on the junior high football team and I was the starting running back and line-backer. Running back was my favorite, because I got to score the touchdowns. On one particular play I was linebacker. I tackled the running back from behind, landing partially on the back of his legs. Somehow I landed on the back of his heel and it pressed into my stomach. It knocked the wind out of me and I lay on the ground for a few moments. As I got up I noticed a sharp pain in my stomach every time I took a breath. I ran to the sideline and tried to shake it off. It was not getting any better but I still finished the game.

After the game I took the bus back to school, showered, got dressed, and walked about a mile home. My mother made dinner, but after eating, it did not sit well with me. I kept on having sharp pains and difficulty breathing. My parents thought to bring me to the hospital to see if I injured my rib. The doctors performed numerous tests and determined I was bleeding internally. I remember my dad signing a consent form for emergency surgery. When I woke up, I had tubes coming out of my nose, mouth, hand, stomach, and groin. The doctors had done exploratory surgery and found that I had ruptured my spleen. As they removed my spleen, it exploded. The doctors told us if I had not gone in that night I would've died in my sleep from internal bleeding. I was one lucky boy to go in that night!

I spent the next seven days in the hospital recovering. Four of those days were spent in the ICU and three days in a room that I shared with a sixteen-year-old named Tom Lewis. Tom was in the hospital dealing with epilepsy, petite and grand mal seizures. Tom and I spent three days together and got to know each other pretty well. He was one of the funniest kids I had ever met! I remember one day a nurse came in to check on Tom as he slept. The nurse tried waking him up to take his temperature, and he inadvertently slapped the nurse in the face, hard. I saw it all happen and I laughed hysterically.

I got a kick out of Tom. He made me laugh a lot during my recovery. The day I was released from the hospital I remember being emotional, shedding a tear as I said good-bye to Tom. He didn't know it but he really helped me out by making me laugh, the best medicine a fourteen-year-old could receive. We didn't keep in touch, but I always wondered about him.

Fast-forward thirty-four years to 2010. I was sitting at Caribou Coffee feeling a bit down, contemplating where I was with my life. I was basically having a pity party! As I sat there, a woman I knew from church, Shawn Lee, came up to me. Shawn is a very positive person who loves the Lord. We said hello and I basically spewed my concerns to her. All I can remember was her advice: "Pray more." Pretty simple. I knew this, but sometimes we get so absorbed with the negatives life can dish out that we can fall into a dark hole. Shawn used two words that snapped me out of my pity party—*pray more*. After she left me, I did pray.

I decided I needed to go to the health club and work out. Working out had become more of an effort because it was difficult for me to get on and off of the machines, plus trying to make it to the bathroom. This particular day I sat on the leather coach watching TV before I went downstairs to work out. I noticed there was a man walking toward me. He sat down next to me. He was sweating profusely, and his trainer was with him and concerned about his health.

At first, I thought I should get up to leave and let him recover. Then something in my mind told me I needed to stay there on the couch next to him. He was struggling trying to gain his breath. I looked at him and something in me (Holy Spirit) prompted me to ask if I could pray for him. I had never asked this question to anyone before in my life. He looked at me and said yes. I asked him his name, and he answered, "Tom Lewis." Instantly I asked if he was from Edina. He said yes. I didn't say a word but closed my eyes and said a prayer for Tom. Moments after that, paramedics came in with a gurney and took Tom away to the hospital. He looked scared but thanked me for praying for him. As he was put into the ambulance, I thought, *I wonder if this is the same Tom Lewis from 1976.*

I asked the trainer working with Tom if I could possibly get his home number to check on him. She did give me his number, and I called him the next day. I was concerned for his health, but I was also very curious if this was the same Tom Lewis that was my roommate thirty-four years ago. I called him and he was home recovering from the electric shock treatment they had given him to slow his heart rate. He thanked me for calling and said everything was under control for right now. I then asked Tom if he was possibly the same Tom Lewis that was my roommate so long ago. He thought about it for a moment and said that he was. I couldn't believe it! I had wondered about this man for many years. I had always wondered what happened to him and was always grateful for how he helped me through that difficult time. Tom and I have reconnected and are a part of each other's lives today! We have spent lots of time together, including a trip to Bethesda, Maryland. I was in a clinical study trial at the National Institutes of Health and Tom was my caregiver.

Shawn Lee, thank you for your advice: pray more! Simple words that can have powerful outcomes.

HELP, I'VE FALLEN AND I CAN'T GET UP

Since I have "retired" (gone on disability), Caribou Coffee has been my so-called office. My made-up name at my office is "Norm." (Remember Norm Peterson from the TV show *Cheers*?) You know, after eight years of sitting in the same location, people tend to know you. I liked it there because of the coffee, I was surrounded by good people, and there was a bathroom nearby! The winter of 2012 was cold and long—nothing unusual in Minnesota. I was using a cane. I have five or six canes, all handmade using different exotic woods. I figured that if I had to use a cane it would be the coolest-looking cane out there. And I wouldn't call them *canes*. They would be my *chick magnets*! They also had unique colors and designs. I was a single man with attitude.

One day as I was coming out of the men's room, I tripped on a mat outside the bathroom. Normal people catch their balance and brush it off like nothing happened. For me, it started a ten-foot stumble. Bouncing off the service counter, I landed facedown, staring at a pair of Cole Haan shoes and dress slacks. The gentleman looked down at me with a smirk and asked if I needed help getting up. I smiled back and said, "Yes, please." I introduced myself to him. Dan Boulay and I have been friends ever since. We sat and talked for the next hour and realized we lived in the same neighborhood and have friends in common. We have created a certain bond you can't make up!

FROM CANADIAN CRUTCH TO WALKER

Another time in 2012, I was sitting at my office (Caribou) having a cup of coffee and journaling. I have found it therapeutic to write down my thoughts and feelings. This coping technique is quite useful and saves money by avoiding having to pay a therapist! Most of my journaling was about my four kids, ex-wife, and whatever drama I was dealing with (girlfriend, health issues, spiritual battles). I actually enjoyed putting everything out there. It felt like I was accomplishing projects and being constructive with my time.

I was using a Canadian crutch at the time, one that your arm goes through a hole and you grab hold of the cane. I walked into the bathroom with one hand on the cane and the other hand closing the door. As I turned to lock the door, my cane tip slipped. My body fell, bounced off the sink, and landed on the bathroom floor. Instantly I was grossed out lying on the bathroom floor. As I tried to push myself up with my hands I noticed a severe acute pain coming from my left wrist. I knew that pain. I could not get myself up with both hands pushing off the dirty floor. There was just too much pain. I turned to my side and reached up with my strong arm and grabbed hold of the door handle. I pulled with all my might and lifted my body up on my feet. I had broken enough bones in my life to know I probably broke my arm.

As I opened the door and left the bathroom, my body went into shock. I sat down at my table and gestured to the ladies working behind the counter that I had injured myself. I rested my head on the table as my armed throbbed. I knew I needed to go to the hospital. I was in no shape to drive myself. I called my brother, David, and he came and took me to the emergency room. After receiving X-rays, they told me I had a spiral fracture in my left wrist. The doctors made a cast for me to wear for the next seven weeks.

This was a big setback. It was no longer safe for me to walk with just a cane anymore. I needed to go deeper into my tool kit and start using a walker. *Oh no! A walker is for much older people who are really disabled. This can't be happening to me, a single forty-nine-year-old man who still has all of his hair, and not gray.* This was very emotionally difficult for me. I thought using a cane made me stand out, but a walker?! I didn't have a choice; what else was I going to do? How was I going to get around? I couldn't just sit in my apartment. I needed to be able to get out and be around people. I decided to put my pride in my back pocket and start using my walker.

KICK ME THREE TIMES

One beautiful summer Sunday in 2012, I pulled into my church parking lot with my Suburban. I parked in the handicapped spot designated for me, the VIP. I got out the front door and was able to hold on to my truck as I walked back to the cargo door to let out "Big Red," my scooter. I had to be very careful holding on to the side of my truck because my balance was not good. As I tried to open up the cargo door, it knocked into me and made me stumble backward and fall into the street. I assessed the situation and knew I was not hurt at all. I felt embarrassed, of course. Who saw me fall? There were plenty of cars pulling into the parking lot. As I lay on my back, I saw a woman and her teenage son walking briskly toward me. They definitely had looks of concern. I knew I had to disarm them. These poor people just witnessed a man fall to the ground and they were scared. As they approached me, I asked them to kick me three times, throw out a couple of snide remarks, and then help me. They were nervous and concerned about my well-being. They looked at me and saw I had a smile on my face, so they began to smile as well. After we introduced ourselves, we began the chore of getting me to my feet and into Big Red. It wasn't pretty, but they got me to church on time. That was three years ago, and Bonny has become a dear friend of mine. I have met her husband and I get to see her and her family at church often and always with big smiles!

WHAT AN ENTRANCE

Later in 2012, on a Friday night I had been out with friends. Dinner and libations. Nothing crazy or out of control. Dealing with MS and drinking alcohol is not the best combination. I like to say "I'm walking around with a six-pack in me all the time!" That night, I parked my Suburban in my underground parking spot. I grabbed my walker from the back seat, pulled it out, locked my truck, and headed to the locked garage door. I have to be careful unlocking and opening the steel door. It is very heavy, and maneuvering through the door is not designed for people like me. I pushed my way through the door using my walker. Well, the walker got ahead of me and I planked. I was stretched out holding on to the walker, and before I knew it I fell to the ground right in front of the elevator. I was on my back, like a turtle, unable to get up. It was after 1 a.m. and I was trapped with a dead cell phone, just lying there with my tipped-over walker. Talk about feeling vulnerable!

When I spend time on the ground after a fall, waiting for ten minutes up to two hours until help arrives, it gives me the opportunity to pray and be grateful. I was grateful that I didn't hit my head or worse. This time I spent about thirty minutes on the ground. I heard a vehicle enter the garage and park. I didn't want to scare the person who would be opening the door. As soon as he saw me, he startled and his eyes got really big. I smiled at him and said, "I'm dealing with MS and fell; could you please help me to my feet?" He was a bigger guy, so he was able to lift my 200 pounds. I introduced myself and told him he was my fifth angel of the day. He got me to my feet as I grabbed my walker. As we rode the elevator up to my floor, I apologized for startling him and thanked him for his kindness.

I really believe there are good things that can come from bad situations. I have learned to keep my eyes off of myself and have them fixed on the Lord. This can be difficult when bad things continually follow you. The book of Job is such a story. He lost pretty much everything—his children killed, his livelihood ruined, and his health under attack. Job had such faith and trust in the Lord, he did not become resentful or angry toward God. Instead, Job leaned into Him and praised Him even more. We have the freedom to choose how we respond to tough times. I have learned how to overcome obstacles that could have put me in the fetal position, sucking my thumb, too scared to live life abundantly.

PLANKING!

Later that same summer I had a date. Her name was Sharon and we had been classmates in elementary and junior high. We had reconnected through friends and had already been on a couple dates before this particular night. My self-esteem was wavering because my MS had been progressing. I decided to take her out for dinner at a local restaurant. I warned her that it was a greasy hamburger joint but that they served great food. She was up for it! At this time with MS I was dependent on using a walker. I arrived early at the restaurant and sat at a table facing the entrance. We greeted each other with a hug and ordered a couple beers. Sharon was going through a divorce, so we had some things in common.

After I finished my beer I excused myself to go to the restroom and began to make my way toward the restroom with my walker. The closer I got, the more I had to go. The door had no handle, so I had to use my walker to push it open. When I did this, it rolled away from me and I planked—my walker extended away from my body and my legs could not catch up to the walker itself. I had been in this position before and it never turned out well. I knew I was about to fall. I braced myself as I crashed to the dirty bathroom floor. My shoe flew off. My walker tipped over. And I still had to pee really, really badly. I struggled to get up. With the weakness of my legs and only one shoe for traction, it was no use.

I decided to crawl to the men's handicap stall, where I thought I could pull myself up using the grab bar. I cringed, knowing how filthy the floor was. I was calling out, "Help me! I've fallen and can't get up!" And I'm thinking that I've got this beautiful girl waiting for me out there, and here I am about to wet myself on the men's bathroom floor. So I did what I normally do in these types of situations. I started praying the Lord's Prayer. I still kept on yelling for help, when finally I heard a woman say, "I hear someone calling for help in the bathroom." As I lay on the bathroom floor starting to really panic, the bathroom door bolted open, and the bartender came flying in. I told him he was my fourth angel of the day as he hoisted me up and set me on the toilet. I thanked God right away!

He gathered my belongings and even put my shoe on my foot as I sat on the toilet. I made it! The whole ordeal lasted about ten minutes but felt like an hour. I made it back to my date grateful and relieved—in more than one way!

YOU CAN DRESS HIM UP, BUT YOU CAN'T TAKE HIM ANYWHERE

That autumn, it was my 50th birthday and a group of friends had gotten tickets for us to see Bruce Springsteen in concert. I really wanted to go! I asked a girl named Jodee to go with me. We were just friends out to have a great time. I wanted to get dressed up. And by dressed up I mean wearing blue jeans and a nice shirt. You see, I wear running pants pretty much everywhere I go. The MS has affected my left hand and I cannot button pants on my own. My occupational therapist taught me how to configure a way to wear my blue jeans without having to put my button in the little hole. I was able to pull up my pants and not have to worry about anything. This trick was fantastic! The night before, I did a trial run putting on my socks, blue jeans, and dress shirt. I put my Cole

Haan shoes on, looked in the mirror, and said, "Damn, you're one good-looking dude," while holding on to my walker. This was the first time I had worn jeans in two years.

It was time. I left my apartment using my walker for assistance. I walked down my apartment hall to the elevator, downstairs to the garage, loaded up my walker into my Suburban, and off I went to pick up my date. I felt really good about myself. I picked up Jodee from the hotel where she was staying and drove to Downtown St.Paul. We were meeting a group of people for cocktails and a light dinner. I pulled into the handicapped parking spot like a VIP, right in front of the restaurant. I had impressed her with the special parking.

The restaurant was partly underground so I needed to use my walker down about five steps to get into the bar section. With Jodee's help, I made it down the stairs without falling. We entered the bar, and it was packed. I was feeling good and looking good, too, I thought. Bruce Springsteen music was playing while people pre-partied for the concert. As I looked around, I noticed I was the only one using a walker. I sometimes notice these things (always). I approached the bar, and numerous friends were there already. Someone handed me a beer and I took a big swallow. This was a lot of work for me.

I stood there trying to relax, holding my beer with one hand and my walker with the other. Having a great time, saying hello to people, I noticed that my pants felt loose. I looked down and my pants had slid down to my knees. My heart dropped. There were people all around me. I panicked! Kelly, a friend of mine who is a nurse, was standing in front of me. Jodee, my date, was behind me. I couldn't let go of the walker to pull up my jeans, because I would fall. So I frantically called (yelled) for Kelly and Jodee to help me and pull my pants up. It was a moment I will never forget. The girls yanked my pants up so firmly and quickly. I think their mothering instincts took over. I was very embarrassed and afraid to take another step but I knew we had a big night and I was all dressed up looking good. Let's have that beer!

DISAPPEARING ACT

MS has affected not only my ability to walk and run but also my bladder control. By 2013, physical urgency had been causing me extreme emotional anxiety, and soon decreased my ability to get around and participate in activities. Going to Jimmy's and Jack's outdoor sporting events needed to be "scouted." Upon arrival, I had to find the closest private spot to relieve myself. I don't think there is a church parking lot I haven't frantically raced into. I could not physically get into a portable restroom by myself anymore. I would open my Suburban doors, stand in between to shield myself, and just go!

From church parking lots, parking ramps and garages, to paths around local lakes and highways. Yes, highways with cars doing 60 MPH flying by me. I remember praying and trusting in the Lord to keep me safe from the speeding traffic. It was a horrible way to live, with day-to-day anxiety over having to use the restroom. It was controlling my life. I had to do something if I wanted to enjoy life while outside my home.

I made an appointment with a urologist. The options were not great, but at least I could help myself. His first advice was to cut out coffee and alcohol. Now, I'm not a big drinker so that was no problem, but cutting out my Caribou Coffee? Well, I did cut back on my intake to only two cups early in the morning. The other option the doctor recommended was self-catheterization. This would be done before I traveled to whatever activity I was attending. The thought of self-cathing was awful. "I can't do this," I said to myself. "There is no way I'm going to be putting that long plastic straw-looking device into my wee-wee!" This was one of the most intimidating, humbling changes that I needed to do. Wait, I take that back. The most intimidating, humbling thing I needed was having a nurse show me how to insert the catheter into my urethra. I now can no longer be embarrassed about anything. This technique took some time to master. But as a result, it usually helps for a couple hours so I can be certain I won't have any urgency issues. This was a game changer for me because it gave me back some freedoms.

The drawback or risk to self-catheterization is that it's easier to develop UTIs (urinary tract infections). I am missing my spleen due to a football injury, so I tend to get infections more easily. I experienced four UTIs in less than a year after beginning this routine. When I get a UTI or any kind of illness, my MS symptoms flare up severely. At first, I notice the skin on my back becomes painful to the touch. The first time this happened I was not aware of what was going on. My body became so fatigued I could not lift my arms or walk at all. We had to dial 911 for an ambulance. When we arrived at the hospital they immediately admitted me and started to work on me. They realized right away I was dehydrated and started an IV. Next they took blood to examine my white blood count and determined my body had an infection. Finally, they determined it was a UTI and added antibiotics to my IV.

This particular time, I was lying in bed in the intensive care unit, getting lots and lots of fluids pumped into me. So after about forty-five minutes, I realized I had to pee. I still was unable to use my arms and legs because the MS flare-up still had a hold of me. It was such a helpless feeling. I told my pretty twenty-five-year-old nurse that I was going to need some assistance. She tried handing me a portable urinal, but I could not grasp it with my own hands. I said, "I'm sorry, but I can't manage this." This had never happened to me before. I had to ask her to assist me by placing my "manhood" inside the urinal. My body was tilted forward in the hospital bed, making it easier to complete the mission. On top of it all, I looked down to see my manhood had disappeared. I looked at my nurse and asked her if she ever watched Seinfeld. She hadn't, so I had to explain that I was dealing with "shrinkage" and that normally I am not so shy. Well, I quickly realized she did not see the humor in my confession. She didn't laugh or even smile. With her latex gloves on, she assisted me. Talk about stage fright! This was another humbling and embarrassing moment that you can't make up. I attempted to use humor to diffuse the awkwardness, but it didn't really work. Not for her. At least I can laugh about it!

LEARNING NEW WAYS

My big white Suburban was easily noticed when I parked in the handicap spot at Caribou Coffee. Friends would see my vehicle and literally take the time to come in and talk with me. They knew my vehicle and they knew this was my hangout spot. I would be about town and strangers would recognize me! I became "the Caribou guy." I guess it could have been worse; I could have been the town drunk hanging out at a bar all day.

My driving was becoming more difficult for me. I used my right foot for pressing on the gas and pressing on the break. Pressing the pedals wasn't the problem. The problem was trying to get my foot to the brake and gas pedal and back again in rapid succession. I would actually use my right hand and lift my leg over to the break or gas pedal. I knew this was unsafe. I knew I needed a driving assessment. I was afraid my license would be revoked, and I wouldn't be able to drive and would lose even more independence.

In 2014, I called the Courage Center to set up a driver's evaluation. As Steve, my instructor, asked me some basic questions to learn more about my issues with driving, I expressed the fact that I have to lift my right leg up and put it on the break and the gas. As soon as I told him this, he told me I should not be driving. My eyes welled up and tears started rolling down my cheeks. I knew this was going to be the answer, but it was so difficult. So, so difficult. I knew I was doing the right thing by being there, but I wanted to leave.

I was not ready for this change in my life. I guess it doesn't matter if you're ready; change just happens. I waited one year before I called Steve back for behind-the-wheel driving lessons with hand controls. I knew I had to. It was becoming more difficult to drive my Suburban. *Safety first* is what I should have been thinking, but that thing called "pride" kept popping up. Resistance to change.

It got to the point where I had to ask friends or strangers walking by for help. They would have to lift my right leg up and shove my butt up onto the driver seat. Once my friends got me settled and the laughter stopped, they would look at me and question if I was okay to drive? I was, but I knew I had to make some changes if I wanted to remain independent.

I called Steve at the Courage Center and set up behind-the-wheel driving lessons with hand controls. He remembered me because we are both former wrestlers and had a lot in common. This was eight hours of learning to drive with your hands only. Parallel parking, getting on and off highways, quick stops—just like when I was sixteen learning how to drive, but this time with my hands and not my feet. It was quite challenging and frustrating. I had to really focus and pay attention to everything that was going on.

It dawned on me that I used to love to drive. Part of my job had been driving across the Dakotas, Minnesota, Iowa, Wisconsin, Illinois, Missouri, Ohio, and Michigan. The driving was treacherous at times—crossing the entire state of North Dakota in the wintertime. Being snowed in 700 miles away from home in Williston, North Dakota. It was all part of being a manufacturer's rep.

It was a Friday when the mechanic installed my new hand controls in my Suburban. IMED Mobility serviced and properly installed the hand controls, custom-made to meet my needs. As I drove out of the parking lot, I felt nervous. Even though I took eight hours of behind-the-wheel training and passed my driving test (on my second attempt), being on my own was nerve-racking. I got onto the highway and headed home.

I stayed in the right lane and drove five miles per hour under the speed limit. My left hand controlled my speed, stopping, and breaking. That's a lot of responsibility to a hand and arm that is affected by MS.

I took my son Jack out that night. We drove to the local softball fields to an event called the Fireman's Tournament. It is a big softball tournament that brings teams in from all over the state—both men and women. I used to play in Fireman's when I was in my twenties. It is very well known in the area and tends to attract people to come back for the weekend, like a reunion. At the end of the evening, with Jack's help, I got into the Suburban. As I was driving and paying extreme attention to my new techniques, Jack said to me, "Dad, it feels like a new car you're driving." That statement made me realize I did the right thing by getting hand controls. He felt safe and and fell asleep on the drive home.

I have underground parking, which is wonderful, always warm and dry. I pushed my remote-control button to enter the garage. I have an end spot, which has more space (width) because of the size of my Suburban. I was pulling in gently to park when my hand pushed forward on the gas, thinking it was the brake. The SUV shot forward and violently hit the brick wall. After the impact, I looked at Jack and asked if he was all right? He was, but he was shook up, and so was I. I felt horrible. His trust in his father's driving abilities had been damaged. We had hit hard. I got out and looked at my SUV. Everything looked fine; nothing was damage, that I could tell.

Jack and I talked later that night, and he told me how good I was driving but that the accident scared him. That really bothered me. The next morning, we got up and Jack needed to get back to his mother's house. As we took the elevator down to the garage he kept questioning my driving. I assured him that it would not happen again; it was an accident on my first day driving with hand controls. As we both got into the SUV, I kept assuring him it would not happen again. Jack sat in the back and we both buckled up.

Parked next to me is a meticulously kept black Lexus. I love cars, so I know the value of that particular vehicle. His car was about six feet away from me on the right while I backed up. I was very careful using my hand controls, aware of every movement I made. As I backed up slowly, I passed a steel beam divider that stands between the two parking spots. The beam is about four feet in circumference. As I backed up, I started to turn my wheels to the right so I could swing out and drive out of the garage. When I started turning and backing up, I thought I had backed out far enough to turn. I realized I had not. I needed to back out farther to turn by the beam. I thought I put the SUV in reverse and was pressing the break with my hand controls. I realized too late that my vehicle was in drive and my left hand was applying the gas.

The truck shot forward, clipping the steel beam and hitting the back end of the Lexus parked next to me. It was a terrible moment. I was thinking to myself that I had installed the hand controls for safety and to be responsible. Instead, I got into two car accidents within ten hours in my underground parking garage. That has to be a record! My truck needed to be towed away; it was not drivable. In fact, it was later determined to be totaled. Needless to say, Jack was terrified to drive with me again.

I wish I could say that was it; that was my last accident. And it was ... with the Suburban.

Three weeks later, I was fitted for a power wheelchair. The MS had progressed more and I was falling quite a bit with my walker. It seems the harder I tried to walk the more difficult it became. The MS, which had been affecting my left leg was now affecting my right leg. This had been a fear of mine for a long time. I was losing my independence! It was no longer safe for me just to use a walker by myself.

The thought of going from walking with a limp, to a cane, to a walker, to a power wheelchair ... Crazy! This is not supposed to be happening to ME! I was strongest and fastest kid in school. I started training in first grade because I wanted to compete in the Olympics or play pro football. My passion was working out and becoming the best athlete I could be.

It's funny, when I was younger I had a fear that maybe one day I might not be able to do all the things that I could do with my body. Things like running, playing golf, working out. I really pushed it when I was younger, doing as much and as many activities as I possibly could. It's quite interesting how things turned out. I am so thankful and grateful that I did all the things I was able to do when I was younger.

Now reinventing myself is the new challenge! Writing this book and speaking in front of people and being a good role model to my kids on handling trials and tribulations – these are the important things. Leading a Christ-centered life and making sure my children know what matters most in life: relationships—with family, friends, and our Lord Jesus. There is a verse in the Bible that I have memorized. James 1:2–3: "Consider it pure joy, my brothers and sisters, whenever you face trials of many kinds, because you know that the testing of your faith produces perseverance."

Coach John Bianchi, "Tiger"

Coach John Bianchi has been in my life since I was about ten years old. John coached me from little league baseball through high school football. John and his wife, Jan, were dear friends of my parents'. Coach Bianchi was my favorite coach throughout my entire athletic career. He possessed the ability to get the best out of me. He used humor to keep things loose and fun, but he had an intensity that would motivate us to run through a brick wall for him. He was great! I remember during football practices he would, from time to time, huddle the offensive unit together and tell us jokes, usually when practice was getting mundane. We were sixteen-year-old boys that were, for the most part, very innocent and naïve. He would get us laughing with slightly off-color jokes and tell us not to tell our parents. We went undefeated that year. I know if you asked the other guys on that team, it was the greatest football season of our lives.

In 1999 John was inducted into the Minnesota Hockey Hall of Fame for his coaching. Recently John was presented a prestigious "Lifetime Achievement Award" named after Cliff Thompson. After forty-five years, coach Bianchi retired from being a principal, teacher, and coach.

John is still a prankster and a jokester, and he usually makes whoever he's with the butt of his jokes. After my dad, then mom passed away, my divorce, and my MS progressing, John was there to help me. He helped me to doctors' appointments, brought meals over that Jan had cooked up, was a committee member of the golf dinner event—the MS Birdie Bash—and most importantly, he was a friend I could talk to and get advice from.

During the summer of 2015, I asked John out for a couple of cocktails to talk about life. When you're with Bianchi, you know there's going to be laughter, and he loves to embarrass you whenever he has the chance. When, after a few cocktails, I needed to relieve myself, I asked John—no, I think I told him—he had to help me, he looked at me and obviously didn't really understand what he was about to experience. I turned on my scooter and off we went to the men's room. John opened the door for me, and we went directly to a bathroom stall. There were a few men using the trough, so it was busy. The stall we entered was a bit tight, but it did have grab bars, so it could be classified as handicapped. John looked at me and asked, "What do you want me to do?" I told John I needed help getting up from my scooter and getting on the seat. As he started to help me, I started to moan loudly and exclaim what soft hands he had. I called him Tiger and told him not to stop! He looked at me and panicked. He opened the stall door frazzled and explained to the guy in the bathroom, "He is just a friend that's handicapped! I'm trying to help! There's nothing going on!" They laughed and I started laughing! After all the years of his ribbing me, I got him back good! John Bianchi is one of a kind, and I have been so blessed to have him in my life.

MEET BILL SCHEIBLER

Bill Scheibler is a man I wish everyone could meet. He served in Vietnam as an Airborne Paratrooper Ranger and was awarded four Purple Hearts and a Bronze Star with Valor. He has seen things no one should ever have to experience. Bill was in the Battle of Ia Drang, one of the bloodiest battles in the Vietnam War. Bill's 186-person unit was down to four survivors, including Bill. He told me, "So many died in my Ranger unit, I feel so fortunate to be one of the few that returned alive." This battle was made into a movie called *We Were Soldiers* starring Mel Gibson and Sam Elliott. Bill and I met in church and have become dear friends. Bill also has MS; in fact, I think he gave me MS in church, passing bread during communion!

Bill has been a very important fixture in my life. He helped me during some difficult times in my life—divorce and the progression of the disease. He taught me how I need to be creative when dealing with the physical and emotional changes of MS. The first is to pray to God and be thankful for all the things we can do.

Bill is a man of integrity and honor, but above all else he is a kind, humble man who gives thanks and praise to the Lord. I want to share Bill with you! Treat yourself and Google "Bill Scheibler.

LUNCH WITH TOMS

In November 2015 I went out to lunch with my dear friend Tom Nunnelly. Tom is now retired, but he had worked in the optical industry his whole life. He owned his own retail store called Optical Studios in Coon Rapids, Minnesota. He and my dad were best friends, and Tom came to a lot of my high school football games and wrestling matches. Tom and I liked to have lunch at Whole Foods in Edina, where the food is healthy and the scenery is...healthy! We have started a tradition of spending time together or lunch one day a week. One particular day we went to Whole Foods for lunch. As Tom was in line paying, as usual, I went to look for a couple seats in the dining area. It's a seat-yourself open area, where you might sit with people you may not know. As I was in my power chair scanning for a place to sit, a gentleman saw me searching and gestured to me that there was space next to him. I rolled over to him and thanked him. As he was finishing his lunch, we introduced ourselves to each other.

His name was Tom McMullen and he was dining alone. After paying, Nunnelly came over with our salads. He introduced himself to my new friend and then helped me get situated to eat. McMullen watched as Nunnelly took my feet off the footplate and rested them on the floor, then adjusted my backrest forward so I don't spill all over myself. Nunnelly then got napkins, a fork, and water for me. McMullen quietly watched how Nunnelly cared for me. The three of us talked for the next hour and had a really nice time. McMullen asked what I did for a living, and I explained that I am on Social Security Disability. I added that I do speaking engagements for the MS Society and raise awareness of MS at schools, churches, and colleges.

Then I told McMullen, "I am trying to write a book, but I get distracted and can't seem to make much progress. I would love to do speaking engagements tied with this not-yet book I want to write." Tom McMullen's eyes got big and he exclaimed, "I can help you! I wrote a book and I know I can help you." Before he committed he said, "Let me get a hold of my friend and my sister. If they can help, you will get your book finished. We exchanged telephone numbers and within two days McMullen called me back and said they were in! It just blows my mind that we all have the capability to make a positive difference in other people's lives by just opening our mouths and communicating.

Tom, thank you so much for meeting with me weekly and holding me accountable. You gently guided me through this process with tender words and an extremely kind heart. I know the Lord placed you in my life. God bless you!

Made in the USA
Lexington, KY
17 February 2018